T0144945

KIDS Kookery A to Z

Kids in the Kitchen for Easy Learning and Fun

Cheryl A Gray

AuthorHouse™
1663 Liberty Drive
Bloomington, IN 47403
www.authorhouse.com
Phone: 1 (800) 839-8640

Published by AuthorHouse 04/05/2019

ISBN: 978-1-5462-7341-7 (sc)
ISBN: 978-1-7283-0763-3 (hc)
ISBN: 978-1-5462-7340-0 (e)

Library of Congress Control Number: 2018915047

Print information available on the last page.

authorHOUSE®

Getting Started

What all Star Chefs should know

* ★ Wash your hands
* ★ Put on your chef's apron and/or hat
* ★ Set up your tools
* ★ Prepare your ingredients
* ★ Follow the recipe
* ★ Take a 'YUMMY' taste test
* ★ Prepare your food for serving
* ★ Give thanks
* ★ Don't forget to clean up

Adults

This cookbook is intended to be used as an interactive way to incorporate FUN and LEARNING between adult and child. Start by looking over the recipe together. Consider how much supervision is required and decide what parts you need to do yourself, what parts the child can do independently, and what parts you can do together. Now get started and most important HAVE FUN!!

APPLE DO'DAHS

TOOLS: measuring cups (½, 1), non-stick cookie sheet, fork, knife, 2 small bowls, 1 medium bowl, rolling pin, measuring spoons (tsp, tbsp), wisk, brush, foil sheet

INGREDIENTS

PASTRY	**1** - box pillsbury refrigerated light and flakey pie crusts
FILLING	**3** - medium apples peeled, cored and diced small, **1/2** - cup brown sugar, **1** – tsp white sugar, **1** - tsp cinnamon, **2** – tbsps soft butter
EGG WASH	**1** - egg white, **1** – tbsp water
GLAZE	**2** - tbsp water, **2** - cups confectioner sugar

INSTRUCTIONS

PREHEAT	the oven at 400°
ROLL	lightly over both pastry sheets making one slightly larger then cut each sheet into 8 equal triangles
LAY	the 8 smaller triangles onto a non-stick cooking pan about ½ inch apart
PEEL	core and dice the apples into small pieces, place in medium bowl and set aside
MIX	the brown sugar, white sugar and cinnamon in a small bowl and blend in the softened butter with a fork
FOLD	the sugar, cinnamon and butter mixture into the diced apples
DROP	the apple filling into the center of each triangle, leave a small edge around all sides of the triangle
LAY	remaining triangles over the apple filled triangles
PRESS	the edges of the triangles together lightly but firmly using a fork
WISK	the egg wash mixture until foamy and brush it lightly over each pastry
MAKE	three small slits in each Do'Dah
SPRINKLE	the tops of your Do'Dahs with a light dusting of white sugar
BAKE	the Do'Dahs in the oven for about 20 minutes (lay a sheet of foil over the top if they are turning too brown)
REMOVE	the Do'Dahs from the oven CAREFULLY and allow them to cool
PREPARE	the glaze mixture and drizzle it over each Do'Dah once they have finished cooling

GIVE THANKS ~ ENJOY ~ CLEAN UP

FUN FINISH: consider serving your Apple Do'Dah with a scoop of vanilla ice cream for a special fun finish

BANANALICIOUS

TOOLS: 8 dessert cups, ¼ measuring cup, medium mixing bowl, cutting knife, mixing spoon

INGREDIENTS

CRUST	**2** - cups graham cracker crumbs
FILLING	**3** - medium bananas, **1** - 16 oz package of banana pudding
TOPPING	**1** - 6.5 oz can whipped cream and vanilla wafer

INSTRUCTIONS

COVER	the bottom of each parfait cup with ¼ cup graham cracker crumbs
SLICE	the bananas and place them in a medium mixing bowl
SPOON	a layer of pudding over the graham cracker crumbs
PLACE	a layer of sliced banana on top of the pudding
SPOON	another layer of pudding on top of the bananas
TOP	each parfait cup with whipped cream and a vanilla wafer

GIVE THANKS ~ ENJOY ~ CLEAN UP

FUN FINISH: consider substituting the graham cracker crumbs
with chocolate cookie crumbs for a special fun finish

CHUNKY CHOCO'S

TOOLS: medium microwave safe bowl, ¾ measuring cup, mixing spoon, cookie scoop, flat cooking sheet, cooking spray

INGREDIENT

1 – 6.8 oz giant hershey's milk chocolate bar with almonds, **1 -** cup cherry craisins, **1** - cup shredded coconut

INSTRUCTIONS

CHOP   milk chocolate bar's into small chunks and place them into a medium microwave safe bowl

MELT   chocolate chunks in microwave for 1-2 minutes, checking every 15 seconds so chocolate does not burn

ADD   craisins and shredded coconut to melted chocolate

MIX   all ingredients together using the mixing spoon

DROP   mixture by cookie scoop onto a cooking sheet which has been covered with cooking spray (makes 12-15)

CHILL   in the refrigerator until firm, about 1 hour

GIVE THANKS ~ ENJOY ~ CLEAN UP

**FUN FINISH: consider serving your CHUNKY CHOCO's in
a foil or paper candy cup for a special fun finish**

DIRT DUMPER

TOOLS: mixer, frosting spreader, 2 medium bowls, 4 mini loaf pans, 2 spoons, cutting knife

INGREDIENTS

TRUCK	**1** - box chocolate cake mix, **1** – 20 oz container red frosting
DIRT	**1** – 22 oz carton vanilla pudding and scooped out cake
FINISH	**16** – mini oreo cookies, **1** – 12 oz bag chocolate M&M's, string licorice

INSTRUCTIONS

PREPARE	the chocolate cake mix as instructed on the box
POUR	the cake batter in to the 4 mini loaf pans
BAKE	your mini loaf cakes as instructed on the box and set aside to cool once done
MEASURE	1/3 back from the front of your loaf then cut 1/3 of the way down and evenly back to the end of your loaf to form the shape of your dump truck and to form a cab on the front end of the loaf
SCOOP	the center out of the back end of your truck and place the scooped cake from each loaf into a medium sized bowl. This creates the dump part of your truck and the scooped cake will be used to make your dirt which will go back into the dump part of your truck
MIX	the vanilla pudding in with the scooped cake which serves as your dirt
SPREAD	your frosting over the cake but do not frost the scooped part of the truck because this is for your dirt
SPOON	the dirt mixture into the dump part of the truck and evenly between each loaf
FINISH	by using the mini oreo cookies for tires, M&M's for your cab beamers and head lights and windows, string licorice for piping

GIVE THANKS ~ ENJOY ~ CLEAN UP

FUN FINISH: consider other variations of cake
and frosting for a different fun finish

EASTER EGGERY

TOOLS: mixer, large mixing bowl, 12-24 cupcake liners, cupcake pan, small bowl, mixing spoon, frosting spreader

INGREDIENTS

CAKE   **1** – box white cake mix
FROST   **1** – 20 oz container white frosting
TOP   **1** – 14 oz bag angel flake sweetened coconut
DECORATE **1** – 14 oz bag mini jelly beans, **1** – 14 oz bag cherry licorice sticks, green food coloring

INSTRUCTIONS

PREPARE   the white cake mix as instructed on the cake mix box, using the cupcake pan and set aside to cool once done
POUR   the cake batter in to the cupcake pans
SPREAD   your frosting on each of the cupcakes using the frosting spreader
FILL   a small bowl with the angel flake coconut, place a few drops of green dye into the coconut and stir until the coconut turns green, roll the top of each frosted cake in the coconut
BEND   a licorice stick, inserting each end into an opposite side of the cupcake to form a handle
LAY   4-6 mini jelly beans in the center of each cupcake

GIVE THANKS ~ ENJOY ~ CLEAN UP

FUN FINISH: consider placing cupcake easter baskets on
a platter of easter grass for a fun Eastery finish

12

FRUIT KABOBS

TOOLS: paper towel, cutting knife, 2 small bowls, 16 kabob sticks

INGREDIENTS

1 – 16 oz can pineapple chunks, **1** – 8 oz jar maraschino cherries, **1** – large apple, **1** – large banana, **1** – 8 oz bag miniature marshmallows

INSTRUCTIONS

DRAIN	juice from the pineapple chunks and maraschino cherries
PLACE	16 pineapple chunks and 16 maraschino cherries on a paper towel
PEEL	the banana and slice into 16 pieces, place them in a small bowl and set aside
PEEL	the apple and slice it into 8 wedges, cut out the core
CUT	each wedge in half for a total of 16 pieces and place them in a small bowl, set aside
LAYER	each kabob stick in the following order: apple wedge, marshmallow, maraschino cherry, marshmallow, banana slice, marshmallow, pineapple chunk

GIVE THANKS ~ ENJOY ~ CLEAN UP

FUN FINISH: consider using other variations
of fruit for a different fun finish

GLAZED CINI BUNS

TOOLS: 13x9x2 inch rectangular cookie sheet, spatula, cutting knife, measuring spoons (tsp, tbsp), measuring cups (1/3, 1 1/3)

INGREDIENTS

BUNS	**1 -** 8 oz refrigerated sheet dough,
	3 - tbsp softened margarine or butter
CINI	**1/3** - cup packed brown sugar, **1 -** tsp ground cinnamon
GLAZE	**1 1/3** - cups powdered sugar, **1 -** tbsp plus **1 -** tsp milk

INSTRUCTIONS

HEAT	oven to 375°
MIX	cinnamon and sugar, set aside
LAY	dough sheet out flat on the cookie sheet
SPREAD	the soft margarine or butter evenly over the dough sheet
SPRINKLE	the CINI mixture evenly over the dough sheet
ROLL	the dough up tightly, starting with the shorter side and lightly tapping the ends to keep them evenly shaped
MOVE	the rolled dough to the center of the cookie sheet
CUT	the dough very carefully into 12 – ½ inch slices and place evenly across the cookie sheet about 1 inch apart
BAKE	10 minutes and remove from the oven
PREPARE	glaze and mix until smooth, drizzle over the warm rolls

GIVE THANKS ~ ENJOY ~ CLEAN UP

FUN FINISH: consider sprinkling raisins or nuts over the dough before rolling it up and baking it

HAM N CHEESE ROLLER

TOOLS: frying skillet, tablespoon, spatula, serving plate

INGREDIENTS

1 – flour or wheat tortilla, **1 -** tbsp margarine or butter, **1** – sandwich cheese slice, **2** – sandwich ham slices

INSTRUCTIONS

HEAT	skillet on medium heat (takes 2-3 minutes, be careful not to overheat the skillet)
LAY	tortilla out flat on a clean surface
PLACE	in the center of the tortilla a ham slice, then cheese slice, then ham slice
ROLL	the tortilla into a tubular shape
PLACE	the butter in the skillet and allow it to melt
LAY	the tortilla onto the buttered skillet and flatten it with the spatula as the cheese begins to melt (about 3 minutes)
TURN	the tortilla over and flatten the other side as well (about 3 minutes), you will begin to see the melted cheese at each end of the tortilla
REMOVE	the tortilla from the skillet and place in on a serving plate to cool before eating

GIVE THANKS ~ ENJOY ~ CLEAN UP

**FUN FINISH: consider using different variations of cheese
and lunch meat for a different fun finish**

ICE DREAMSICLE

TOOLS: ice-cream scoop, baking sheet. baking sheet, 1 - tablespoon

INGREDIENTS

CONES   **24 -** ice cream cones
CAKE   **1 -** box white cake mix
TOPPING   **1 -** carton vanilla ice cream
FINISH   **1 -** jar of orange tang

INSTRUCTIONS

PLACE   each cone into a cupcake pan
PREPARE   cake mix following the directions on the box
POUR   1 heaping tablespoon of cake mix in to each cone, they will be about half full
BAKE   the cones in the oven following the directions on the box (be careful not to over
           bake, if you insert a toothpick into the cupcake it should come out clean)
COOL   the baked cones
SCOOP   the ice cream and place one large scoop on the top of each cone or two if you
           prefer
SPRINKLE   the top of each cone with orange tang

GIVE THANKS ~ ENJOY ~ CLEAN UP

FUN FINISH: consider topping each cone with whip cream
and an orange slice for an extra Dreamy Finish

JIGGLY 'O'

TOOLS: medium bowl, 10-12 round jello molds

INGREDIENTS

JELLO
1 – 6 oz packet lime jello,
1 – 20 oz can pineapple rings,
1 – 8 oz jar maraschino cherries
TOPPING
1 - can whip cream

INSTRUCTIONS

PREPARE
jello mix in the bowl following the directions on the box

PLACE
'O' pineapple rings at the bottom of each round mold

PLACE
a maraschino cherry in the center of each **'O'** pineapple ring

POUR
jello mixture over the **'O'** pineapple rings, just until each is covered

STORE
the jell**'O'** molds in the refrigerator until set and JIGGLY, about 6 hours

REMOVE
the jell**'O'** from each mold, placing each on a dessert saucer

TOP
each jiggly jell**'O'** with whip cream

GIVE THANKS ~ ENJOY ~ CLEAN UP

FUN FINISH: consider topping each jiggly jell'O' with a
little lime zest for a jiggly jell'O' tart finish

KABOBER STICKS

TOOLS: knife, plate, small bowl, serving platter

INGREDIENTS

24 - pepperoni rounds, **24 -** cheese rounds or squares,
24 - pitted whole black olives, **12 –** dipping pretzel sticks

INSTRUCTIONS

CUT   a small x in the center of each pepperoni and each cheese, place them on a plate and set aside

DRAIN   the black olives and place them in a small bowl, set aside

LAYER   each pretzel stick in the following order: 1 olive, 1 pepperoni, 1 cheese, 1 pepperoni, 1 olive

PLACE   the finished kabober sticks on the serving platter

GIVE THANKS ~ ENJOY ~ CLEAN UP

**FUN FINISH: consider serving the Kabober Sticks with
a cup of tomato soup for a fun lunch finish**

LEMONY CRAN SPARKLE

TOOLS: 2 qt pitcher, cutting knife, juicer, measuring cup (1)

INGREDIENTS

4 – medium lemons, **1 -** cup white sugar, **3 -** cups cold water, **3 –** cups cranberry ginger ale

INSTRUCTIONS

FIRMLY	roll the lemons across a counter top
CUT	the lemons in half and juice each half
POUR	the lemon juice in to the 2 quart pitcher, being careful to remove all lemon seeds
ADD	1 cup sugar, 3 cups cranberry ginger ale and 3 cups cold water to the pitcher
STIR	until the sugar is completely dissolved
SERVE	over cubed or crushed ice

GIVE THANKS ~ ENJOY ~ CLEAN UP

FUN FINISH: consider replacing the ginger ale with strawberry
7 up for a strawberry delicious fun fresh finish

Mac and Cheesier

TOOLS: 2 large pots, measuring cup (1 ½), teaspoon

INGREDIENTS

1 - pound of your favorite macaroni, **1 ½** - cups half and half, **½** - pound velveeta cheese (room temperature), **4** - ounces cream cheese, **8** - ounces sharp cheddar cheese

INSTRUCTIONS

BOIL	water in a large pot
ADD	macaroni and cook, about 7 minutes
STRAIN	reserving 1 cup of the pasta water, set aside
HEAT	the half-and-half in a large saucepan over medium heat until it just comes to a simmer
ADD	cream cheese and velveeta cheese, stir until melted
WHISK	in the cheddar until all the cheese is melted and the sauce is smooth
COMBINE	the macaroni and cheese sauce
STIR	in some of the reserved pasta water to thin the sauce, if needed
OPTION	save ½ cup cheddar cheese to sprinkle on top and bake for 10 mins at 350° until cheese is melted and brown on top

GIVE THANKS ~ ENJOY ~ CLEAN UP

FUN FINISH: consider adding diced tomato and
¼ cup of salsa for a zesty fun finish

NUTTERY BANANA POPS

TOOLS: 3 baking sheets or square pan's, roll of plastic wrap, freezer container, 12 popsicle sticks

INGREDIENTS

12 - peeled bananas, **1** - jar peanut butter, **1** - container hershey's chocolate syrup, **1** - bag crushed peanuts

INSTRUCTIONS

SPREAD	peanut butter on bottom of baking sheet or square pan
SPREAD	chocolate syrup on bottom of baking sheet or square pan
SPREAD	crushed peanuts on bottom of baking sheet or square pan
ROLL	bananas in peanut butter, then chocolate syrup, then crushed peanuts
WRAP	bananas in plastic wrap
LAY	nutty banana in a freezer container and place them in the freezer until frozen
REMOVE	the nutty banana pops from the freezer
FINISH	push a popsickle stick through one end of the banana and it is now ready to eat

GIVE THANKS ~ ENJOY ~ CLEAN UP

**FUN FINISH: consider replacing the chocolate syrup
with caramel for a delectable fun finish**

OAT AND CHOCO CHIP COOKIES

TOOLS: cookie sheet, mixing bowl, measuring cups (¼, ½, 1), measuring spoons (tsp, tbsp) mixing spoon,

INGREDIENTS

1 - cup butter or margarine, softened, **1** - cup packed light brown sugar, **2** - eggs, **1** - teaspoon vanilla extract, **1 ¼** - cup self-rising flour, **3** - cups quick cooking oats, **1 ½** - cup semisweet chocolate chips

INSTRUCTIONS

PREHEAT	the oven at 325°
MIX	together brown sugar and butter in a mixing bowl until it forms a cream consistency
BEAT	in one egg at a time
STIR	in vanilla extract
BLEND	flour into creamed mixture
MIX	in oats and chocolate chips
DROP	by heaping tablespoonful onto ungreased cookie sheets
PLACE	in preheated oven and bake between 20-23 minutes
REMOVE	cookies from the oven and allow them to cool

GIVE THANKS ~ ENJOY ~ CLEAN UP

FUN FINISH: consider adding pecan pieces for a nutty fun finish

P B&J PIZZA

TOOLS: tablespoon, flat cooking sheet, pizza cutter, spreader, small bowl

INGREDIENTS

1 - flat bread, **2** – tbsps smooth peanut butter, **2** – tbsps grape jelly

INSTRUCTIONS

PREHEAT   the oven at 350°
MIX   peanut butter and jelly in small bowl
LAY   the flat bread on the cooking sheet
SPREAD   the peanut butter and jelly mixture evenly over the flat bread
BAKE   the flat bread for approximately 10 minutes or until the peanut butter and jelly is warm through and through

GIVE THANKS ~ ENJOY ~ CLEAN UP

FUN FINISH: consider stacking one pizza on top of another then using a cookie cutter for a fun cut out finish

UESADILLA

TOOLS: medium non-stick skillet, cutting knife, spatula, one small bowl, one medium bowl

INGREDIENTS

8 - 10 inch flour tortillas, **1** - medium tomato, **1** - 8 oz pkg shredded mexican cheese blend, **1** - 8 oz shredded monterey cheese, **1** - 6 oz jar salsa, cooking spray

INSTRUCTIONS

LAY	the tortillas out on a clean and flat surface
MIX	cheeses in a medium bowl and set aside
DICE	tomato and place in a small bowl
PLACE	diced tomatoes evenly across one half of each tortilla
PLACE	cheeses evenly across one half of each tortilla
COAT	a medium size non-stick skillet with cooking spray
PREHEAT	the skillet over medium-high heat until warm
PLACE	one tortilla in skillet and cook 1 minute or until the bottom of the tortilla is golden
FOLD	tortilla in half, cook 30 seconds or until cheese melts
REPEAT	procedure with remaining tortillas
CUT	each quesadilla into 4 wedges and top with salsa

GIVE THANKS ~ ENJOY ~ CLEAN UP

FUN FINISH: consider topping with a dab of sour cream for even more of a fiesta fun finish

RED WHITE AND BLUE CAKE

TOOLS: 8x10 cake pan, mixing bowl, mixing spoon

INGREDIENTS

COAT	cooking spray
CAKE	**1 -** white cake mix
COLORING	red, white, blue food coloring
FROSTING	**1** - 12 oz cool whip
DECORATE	**1** - pint fresh blueberries
	1 - quart fresh strawberries, sliced

INSTRUCTIONS

COAT	cake pan bottom and sides with cooking spray and lightly flour
MIX	the white cake mix as instructed on the box
POUR	the white batter in to the cake pan
DROP	2-3 drops of each color food coloring on the cake batter and use a knife to carefully swirl the colors through out the batter
BAKE	the cake as instructed on the box
SET	the cake aside to cool
FROST	the cake with cool whip
PLACE	the blueberries on the cake to make the stars and the sliced strawberries on the cake to make the stripes

GIVE THANKS ~ ENJOY ~ CLEAN UP

FUN FINISH: Serve the cake with sparkler candles for a patriotic fun finish

SSSSSSSSTRAWBERRY SHORTIES

TOOLS: flat cookie sheet, bowl, mixing spoon, medium bowl, 12 serving dishes

INGREDIENTS

SHORTIES	**1 -** can large fluffy biscuits
TOPPING	**1 -** 8 oz thawed sliced strawberries
TOPPING	**1 -** pint fresh strawberries, sliced
TOPPING	**1 -** can whipped cream

INSTRUCTIONS

SLICE	the fresh strawberries, place in medium bowl and set aside
MIX	the thawed strawberries in with the fresh sliced strawberries
PLACE	the strawberries in the refrigerator until needed
PREPARE	the can biscuits as instructed on the can
REMOVE	the biscuits from the oven and set them aside to cool
BREAK	the cooled biscuits in half
PLACE	the bottom of each cooled biscuit in individual serving dish
POUR	half of the strawberries evenly over the 12 biscuit halves
PLACE	the top half of the cooled biscuit in each serving dishes
POUR	the remaining half of the strawberries over the 12 biscuit tops
TOP	each of the 12 biscuits with whipped cream

GIVE THANKS ~ ENJOY ~ CLEAN UP

FUN FINISH: consider replacing the biscuits with shortcakes for another fun shortie finish

TACO CRUNCH AND MUNCH

TOOLS: skillet, knife, measuring cup, med bowl, large serving bowl

INGREDIENTS

1 - lb ground beef, **1** - pkg (1 ¼ oz) taco bell seasoning mix, **1** - cup water, **1** - head of chopped iceberg lettuce, **1 ½** - cup shredded mexican cheese blend, **1** - cup french dressing, **1** – 8 oz dorito chips

INSTRUCTIONS

CRUNCH	doritos and place in large serving bowl, set aside
CRUMBLE	meat and brown it in the skillet, drain grease
STIR	in seasoning mix and water, simmer on low heat for 5-10 minutes
CHOP	up the lettuce, place in a bowl, set aside
POUR	finished meat over the doritos
MIX	in cheese, dressing, lettuce
SERVE	immediately

GIVE THANKS ~ ENJOY ~ CLEAN UP

FUN FINISH: consider trying different flavors of dorito chips for many surprise fun finishes

UPPSY DOWNSY TURNSY PINEAPPLE N BERRY CAKE

TOOLS: measuring cups (¼, ½, 1), bundt cake pan, small bowl, medium bowl, table knife

INGREDIENTS

¼ - cup coconut oil, **1** - cup mixed berry seltzer water, **1** – whole peeled and chopped pineapple, ½ – pint fresh blueberries, **1** - box yellow cake mix

INSTRUCTIONS

PREHEAT   oven to 350°

SPRAY   cooking oil on bottom and sides of bundt cake pan

CHOP   pineapple on the cutting board and place it into a medium bowl

WASH   the fresh blueberries and mix them in with the pineapple

PLACE   half of the fruit mixture onto the bottom of the bundt cake pan

POUR   half of the dry cake batter on top of the fruit mixture

PLACE   the remaining fruit mixture on top of the cake batter

MIX   the remaining dry cake batter with the seltzer water and pour over the fruit mixture

DRIZZLE   the coconut oil on top of the cake mix, puncture holes in the cake mix

BAKE   the cake for about 37 minutes

GIVE THANKS ~ ENJOY ~ CLEAN UP

FUN FINISH: consider adding a spoonful of whipped cream on the top of each serving for a scrumptious fun finish

VALENTINE COOKIES

TOOLS: rolling pin, heart cookie cutters, flat baking sheet, serving platter, frosting spreader

INGREDIENTS

1 – box of sugar cookie dough, **¼** – cup flour, **1** – 16 oz can of pink frosting, white and red heart candies, measuring cup (¼)

INSTRUCTIONS

PREPARE   the sugar cookie dough as instructed on the cookie dough package, set aside

DUST   a clean surface with flour and roll out the cookie dough

CUT   the cookie dough in to heart shapes using the cookie cutter

PLACE   the cookies on a flat baking sheet and bake as instructed on the cookie dough package

REMOVE   the sugar cookies from the oven and set them aside to cool

FROST   cooled cookies with pink frosting using the frosting spreader and place them onto the serving platter

DECORATE   each cookie with the white and red heart candies

GIVE THANKS ~ ENJOY ~ CLEAN UP

FUN FINISH: use a heart shaped cookie cutter to shape the cookies into hearts

WIENIE ROLL

TOOLS: cooking sheet, knife

INGREDIENTS

24 - cocktail size smoked link sausages (14 oz pkg), **1** – 8 oz can refrigerated crescent dinner rolls

INSTRUCTIONS

HEAT	oven to 375°
UNROLL	can of dough and separate the triangles
CUT	each triangle lengthwise into 3 narrow triangles
PLACE	sausage on longest side of each triangle
ROLL	to the opposite point
PLACE	sausage on ungreased cookie sheet
BAKE	12 – 15 minutes until golden brown
REMOVE	sausages immediately from cookie sheet

GIVE THANKS ~ ENJOY ~ CLEAN UP

FUN FINISH: serve dipping sauces on the side such as ketchup, mustard, barbeque sauce for a dippity do dah finish

X'S AND O'S

TOOLS: cookie sheet, measuring cup (1), frosting spreader, piping bag

INGREDIENTS

1 - 16.5 oz – refrigerated sugar cookies, **1** - cup vanilla frosting, **1** - cup chocolate frosting

INSTRUCTIONS

PREPARE   sugar cookies as instructed on the package
REMOVE   the cookies from the oven and cool for 20-30 minutes
SPREAD   the vanilla frosting over the sugar cookies
PLACE   the chocolate frosting in the piping bag
PIPE   the chocolate frosting over the cookies, half in the shape of an X and half in the shape of an O

GIVE THANKS ~ ENJOY ~ CLEAN UP

FUN FINISH: decorate the tops with sprinkles
for a colorful X's and O's fun finish

YOGURT PARFAIT

TOOLS: knife, 2 small bowls, serving spoon, parfait cups, measuring cup (1)

INGREDIENTS

1 - 20 oz container of plain vanilla yogurt, **1** – pint fresh strawberries, **1** – pint fresh blueberries, **2** – cups granola

INSTRUCTIONS

SLICE	the strawberries and place them in a small bowl, set aside
FILL	the parfait cups half way with yogurt using your serving spoon
PLACE	a layer of the blueberries and sliced strawberries in to each parfait cup in equal portions
FILL	the parfait cups with the remaining yogurt using your serving spoon
SPRINKLE	granola on the top of each yogurt parfait

GIVE THANKS ~ ENJOY ~ CLEAN UP

FUN FINISH: consider other fruit and
granola variations for more fun finishes

ZEBRA STRIPE CUPCAKES

TOOLS: large mixing bowl, cupcake pan, serving platter, frosting spreader, spoon, sandwich bag, scissors

INGREDIENTS

1 – box white cake mix, **1** – 20 oz container white frosting, **1** – 20 oz container chocolate frosting

INSTRUCTIONS

PREPARE	the chocolate cake mix in the large mixing bowl as instructed on the box
POUR	the cupcake batter in to the cupcake pan
BAKE	the cupcakes as instructed on the box and set them aside to cool
REMOVE	the cooled cupcakes from the pan and place them on the serving platter
SPREAD	the white frosting on to the top of the cooled cupcakes using the frosting spreader
SPOON	the chocolate frosting in to a sandwich bag
CUT	the tip of one corner of the bag with scissors
SQUEEZE	the frosting through the open tip and gently glide your hand back and forth over the cupcakes to create zebra stripes

GIVE THANKS ~ ENJOY ~ CLEAN UP

**FUN FINISH: consider a layered white and black cake to achieve
your zebra stripes as a different creative finishes**

Cooking Tools

Bundt Cake Pan

Cooking Mitt

Cupcake Pan

Flat Cookie Sheet

Hand Wisk

Kabob Sticks

Measuring Cup

Measuring Spoons

Mini Loaf Pan

Mixing Bowls

Mixing Sticks

Round Cake Pan

Spatula

Printed in the United States
By Bookmasters